Pauper Estate

Also by Andrew Duncan

Knife Cuts the Water (Poetical Histories, Cambridge, 1990).
Cut Memories and False Commands (Reality Studios, 1991).
From the Kitchen Floor (Microbrigade, London, 1992).
Sound Surface (Wiwaxia, London, 1992).
Alien Skies (Equipage, Cambridge, 1993).
Skeleton Looking at Chinese Pictures (Waterloo Press, 2000).
Switching and Main Exchange (Shearsman, Kentisbeare, 2000).
Pauper Estate (Shearsman, Kentisbeare, 2000).

PAUPER ESTATE

Andrew Duncan

Shearsman Books
2000

*First published in Great Britain in 2000
by Shearsman Books,
Lark Rise, Fore Street, Kentisbeare, Cullompton, Devon EX15 2AD.*

*Distributed in the U.K. by Oasis Books, 12 Stevenage Road, London SW6
6ES and Peter Riley (Books), 27 Sturton Street, Cambridge CB1 2QG.*

*and in the U.S.A. by:
Small Press Distribution, 1341 Seventh Street, Berkeley, CA 94710.
Email: orders@spdbooks.org
Website: http://www.spdbooks.org*

*Printed and bound at The Book Factory, 35-37 Queensland Road,
London N7 7AN.*

ISBN 0 907562 28 0

Acknowledgements
Some of these poems first appeared in *Oasis, 10th Muse* and *Gare du Nord*.
My thanks to the editors.

Contents

dedicated to Luciana Bocchino

The transformation of everyday life

Historicity is because we mimic each other, the fluid external
To the archaic strophes nobly repeated from stopped to steady.
And the problem of time's non-identity is not helped
By the order in which sounds arrive, in a walled garden
Where the industries of seeing and editing catch
The non-contrastive tints that fall from east to west, each
With a proper music, one hop from the nearest star,
For facing the era of mass intellectual originality.
The colourman on the serotonin tap mingles seriatim
Like states of one print called *the structures of everyday life*,
An aura of red and white, bleeding on soft paper, concentric, in a shell
Flushing the entries of the day: she says *vividness* is not *reflexivity*.
Or, trying to separate a woman from her clothes
Newton's mantle trimmed and flounced by Maradan
More precisely, bought in a fair fight at the Static Motif sale.
Although the house belongs to someone else
What I desire is what I am perceiving and the offset
Falls out to re-geometrise me as implicit.
The woman I love tiptoeing into a fig-tree
When suddenly—

You don't love me any more? I can't love you?
You're in love with an ardent man of high ideals
Who can't leave his girlfriend? she would be too unhappy?
You share this ideal? all your promises expired?
This beautiful woman is in distress, I work on a way
Of cajoling fate to bring the union of lovers.

the breadth of my face no longer widens your eye
dissolves back into coarse eyebrows, cheeks, bulge
of forehead, so many numbers in the depot yard
where millions exhibit a common flesh

You implore him to leave you to prove his ethical height?
You drop me over the side to keep this nobility in the air?
You lie awake for a week tossing, not without racinian delight,
Insoluble decisions, and by day ask me to settle them?
Honour demands that you break faith to reach love, I say;
You have the chance of sacrificing love to save honour,
And in general there is a lot of Hegel about.

a world diagram where I am three drops
of colour in cell (8,8)
that are shivered
and wiped away.
Your judgement, who am I to fault it?

Weeping beauty, horror, transcendence, ill with cold
And strain—it's my fault? if I could have been stayed in love with
The tragedy would have flopped? I'm unreliable because you walked out?
I don't own a car, a house, a revolution, or a Theory?
You don't want to go on living? I have to do the shopping?

a shell rooted to a rock, an open valve
where hands, gut, nerve ganglia, genitals
grow into shape inches across
and eat each other up again
detachments in a grey pulsing mass

Shake

My voice
Is an insect pecked off my eye by a bird
That flies to my street
And snaps it up with a tilt of the head and an audible clack.
Words in my mouth like sour cloying mash
That cannot spit or swallow.
I separate myself from the pain and it says, You aren't educated enough
To know what these people aren't saying.

A social standing, a set of authorised actions
A stock of verbal coins, an ego-archipelago
Of symbolic props and agreed memories
Twist through the bird's craw into their new shape.

A clay golem that ties brooms
And begs for eyes
A bad servant that soils precious loads
And never says clever things

An eye opened onto me
It became me and I reflected it, a flutter of second-long symmetries
As it adjusted the screens to my non-existence.
Distinctions too fine for my senses
Carry the commands, and the space I vanish from
Becomes the zone where rules are made and played out.
I dig my tilting house a new footing
In a blood gully, rat hole, hollow stream, moral flaw.

An open shell
Where dwarf human organs grow and eat each other
And spill their contents, and grow.
Volumes of air linking three people in a garden
I drink my fill of and swallow gushing
A red pipe down which the inside of my body
Pours in a rush that swirls and shakes
To a strange static tune.

Violent rays
Where the glittering eyes loop searching for a vacant body.
Returning light maps a world of objects,
Spikes and surges open the count of new organs.

Snow-puffed plumage

A Siberian wilderness turns, a thousand sleigh days on-end

to draw me into the space that has no danger
where gluts of energy vanished in their utterance
to a plane climax of effacement, that spaces out

monotony to nip in ideas their sonance
of hurt, stitching a night like toxic green stars;
sloping walls where each grain falls back and in.

Solitude takes the wanting out of want, love
sheathed in a blue heat signature, neutral, to
match the alien, in plump kilograms of old wool,

disuses this distending and narrowing in,
does not open on the rich, volatile, and piquant;
to live aimlessly and die obscurely.

The Speaking Head

The dusk of waking groups as the loved and cursing Speaking Head,
oral and flower-eyed, in dialogues that joy made captive, she
pours away the evidences of her clemency
and as a philosopher adjuring a court she destroys
his looks and deeds and discovered assets. He counter-pleads, losing footing
in a spiral of shouts and faintness. What his containing skin contained
is on the floor as offal and chat and grey-skinned water.
As sound leaves his insides hurt. Get up and put your clothes on then,
it's morning.

He starts to stand in the post office, at the back of three loops,
in a wash of CC-TV ads. Notices his landlady.
There is a matter of three years unpaid rent.
Buys a padded envelope. Leaves again. She
follows him into the street, catches him up. Is he
going to pay the money? Mime of vagueness, anger, fear, shame, and politeness.
Despair. Is he going to get a job? is he going
to move out? While he is living at the expense of an old woman,
his dependants have picked up their stakes.
She felt great affection for him because of his love of Russia,
his shelves of Slavic poets. Phonecalls, then, in her mother tongue.

And walks six miles south to meet the Speaking Head. Beyond the house
filled with the sound left by a child weeping
two voices lead anger and the birth of solitude away
by means of a big green curve of hill,
paired calm and loving parents mix panic down
in a household bowl of flurry and carry away and taking part
in the cold of an evening where skaters roll by.

Rare extent of dusk above the swings in the playground

Slowly departs from love as the wrap of sleep's deep
tolerant hollow folds tight.

Unrecoverable truths by an authority on morals,
the Medusa opens the count of his old friend, divorced,
three children under six, tells him to marry her.
"For me no sex, no romance. Just skivvying
for someone else's children." She lays proofs
of his irrational selfishness in loving one person,

consequent loss of claims to be loved by her
on the table like banknotes.

Train rush of big emotions shivering words with
turbulence like wings, wilder and more shaking than
articulate sound. Recesses of a house filled
with pain for which there is no moment. Vomiting out rage
to gain reason, eating it up again
to gain strength. Throwing it up again
to reach sleep. Violent embrace to mend an aching head.

The realisation that she is not the same as the person she loves
physically offered by a room kept empty but for the slats of a bed
where she goes to leave the faces, the voices, and the feelings
and hear the no-one's words that live in that room.
The warehouse by the big transit road that sells serially
objects of reproach, conflict, oscillation, betrayal,
for the Dark Room and the offices of revolt and introspection,
pedagogic ordeal which all three compete for
several feet away from the company and its graces of equity.

At the Lido

In months of practice, living for one chance,
I frame and address to a woman who has lived
swallowing the words of men,
their parallel cities of cooled ceramic planes, their
shores of the happiness of women; her
eyes dilated by their magnificence, counting
their points like a cavalry general at a horse fair,
like a restaurateur at the five o'clock market,
so roused with rage and delight and exhaustion—
such true and clinching words that die
on the brink of their office, in a slide
of syllable stubs, glowering white while others
declaratively and in jurally binding form
dissolve the errors of urbanism and sexuality.

Paired and stretched by draughting devices
I was set out as an outline on a wall
its cells extending as a grid: as the boundary faded
I swung back out of the world,
as hands effaced or retraced the shape that bound me
—following a measurement of ancestry or prestige—
I swung between light and darkness
time falling from my limbs in white drops.
Should I re-animate this low-status male
or slip into the bodiless pattern of Gwion,
who looks at a thousand stones and remembers each one
as a cipher of transcendence.
Not knowing rage and satiation, he fills a room
with painted stones, and makes new patterns
for days on end, giving a name to each one.
The strings of the eyes are not worn through
the light of the nearest star falls dappled and unimpaired
through leaves and birds in bursts to wash the household words.

Holden Road. Patched porous and coarse hewn.
Yellow honeycomb aerated composite cake infill
compacted slag and furnace slacks
clenched by mortar as if by yellow horse teeth
big headed purple clinker blackened with soot.
Grosse oeuvre filled in with circles and lozenges of bricks
the best wall in Barnet

irregular and deep, unhewn,
topped by blue coving.

A child ritual where I bury the decaying flesh of a pear
and return to dig up a cylinder of bright unpitted metal
a verb indicating a gesture with teeth and wrists, a figure of three people.
A limb with which they control larger kites and suction cleaners
used under clear water.

Walk past the Council land along Regent's Park Road
Territorial Army depot, multiplex cinema, football ground,
large-scale divisions of space,
school, rubbish dump, motorway, woodland.
The closed coldwater pool at Finchley Lido,
two hours of swimming made your skin very cold and freckled
and then two of sex made it very warm and pink
as the fluid inside went all happy.

Fall of gulls
                the ruffled limbs
                                planing onto green
The waters inside and outside
                                curved masses slip-strike
                                                in cool smooth flow
Forelimbs scissor and flick
                        seagull glide over water
                                        my arms ruffle and fletch
Swipe and kick
                fall of gulls
                        white draft on blue
Turn and glide
                four blade fluid drive
                                wet masses clasp
My image and flow
                soar of gulls
                        stiff bank of oars
Little ripples lap
                back rakes pinions and eases
                                sift and hiss of surf
Roll and sluice back
                fluency chilled buoyancy
                                gulls land and fold
Embraced and suspended
                soar on crystal plume
                                precise crash uplifted

Gasp slap and dash
              hail clutch of gulls
                             drop grips of breeze and sunlight
Arc of wingtips flicks
               world of roofs beneath
                             sharp tumbling eye
Fall of gulls
            blade runs down sheer curtain
                          a flick of the wrist arrests
Cold skin changes colour
                wake swashes back as cylinder
                          swimmer echoed as water walkers

A kind of sound from a vibrating surface with two perforations
A substance obtainable from rosehips and the feathers of birds
A bilateral gripping object for making scrolls
Figures on the roof of a
Clay booth-shrine with chevrons, band of wave peaks, and a stripy cat.

A file that allows colour vision and detection of volumes.

Why didn't I pour love
into jars with airtight lids
so I could have it now it's gone?

A barrow on a busy street
where a trader with a round face
and teeth made of wood
offers a refined-looking woman
a soiled item straight from stock, "Lady,
it's about the wild erotic play
of a refined-looking woman and a sensitive man.
She's got clear white skin
He's got big bright eyes.
Just look at that clear white skin!
These two don't care what they do."
She would never read that kind of story
She's read that story a hundred times.

Small animals don't bother with territories,
they just reproduce as fast as they can and then die.

Least Energy Structures

Sealed compacted mud where heat is dead.
Full fall where way is none.
Flooded passageways and davits. Flush with resting bed. Plates gripped by
[balks of water.
Lading of sisal, tins of pineapple, coffee beans, sunflower seeds, ingot copper
[and zinc

whose threads of decay off northwest Spain
beacon to the larvae of the worm lamellibranchia,
from untheorised crustal seeps under European waters,
where migrants carried phonetic structures;
they grid the sea, to grow internal Time where the
voice aqualandscape
is the foreknown place singing as drops on its skin.
From passive drift acquiring new organs

a lowest energy structure
of tiles with imaginary colours
liquid falls into the rules of geometry
a safe arrangement of my objects
the state of cooling where cooling can no longer occur
no adjacent space involves change
no symmetries to acquire flaws

a lattice of vacancies and impurities

Larval intelligence of one situation only
a ghost star-reckoning by nuzzling a trace
richness of the waters, rarefying as the cube of distance,
radio waves dissipating beyond the moon.
Travels at the surface where the light water spins,
diving when the contaminants say *here*
by an adjustment of internal pressure.

A body even in every direction
that cannot be split
imitating, never incorporating.

Drawn by a lack,
I walk carefully in complete circles
guided by cellular want marking the skin of my face

a self-repairing pattern
strained by the imperatives of symmetry

I chew the full organs of plants and animals,
proteins dismantling proteins with a knife of three-dimensional tiles.
Where membranes set a chemical break,
The I as a frequency curve, in a space of curves, a
lethality rule towards minor distributions,
a pattern that engorges other patterns,
an asymmetry in time which
pays itself back.
My rules
to filter spoil along a cascade of centrifuges
perspectivally towards a climax
the one-way spiral, safe from recursions.

before phonemes. a border
where both sides are alike
and the boundless has the structure of a bed ooze

ash of apricot wood. ash of scenography. ash of a silk slip.

Glass losing equable temper

As the sound expands and fades to a caught breath
the panel award me a mop
I stoop, and splash around our feet
my far and wide passages of knowledge
my network of admirers and imitators.
Draining out sentiments of possession
have the shape of a body: swollen and tenuous
in coloured curling plumes, as cold seeps inward.

Cut to the presidial session, go to the detailed sound.
To the even night where the flareless moonlight
chills colours out of clear forms, and organs
cool into their stations. It took seconds of my life,
swipe the traces on my eyes and skin that wash away.
bed them in cotton wool, lay them in their cabinet.

Partition of magnificently paused syllables,
equable working through divided obligate form,
smooth cerebral switching of bad heats to a periphery,
slow moving through the noble trees hung in green.
The *Aeneid* does not lose a foot when you expel calm.

Consort to a woman who was
—artistically, economically, even sexually—
my superior, I was wealthy in her
as she was measuring me
—intellectually, socially, morally,
as a companion
and spout of *décousu* happy chatter—
to find
            her possession of me
                            a test of poverty.
I saw her tip
            the paper cone of wet coffee grounds
                            into the bin with the leavings
And I knew
            who was going with them.
Her set cast of mind
            dividing fine divisions as coarse
                            was superior and sad,

The melancholia
        of the conductors of philosophy
                who see flaws in joy
As she tracked in rare texts
        the faultless paces
            which compose a high life
She weighed out the one she loved
        in scales made of moths' wings
           calling the invisible to quiver a hair.
As if my skin were a grater
        and my delusions gross and thin
           she recounts my inadequacies all day.

Scaling of space
        as my hand
           moves across her breast
Elm row of time
        as I woke and after 1/10 second
             remembered she loved me.
Time like a ceramic,
        so smooth and calmly curved
             back on itself through
The blue night's red core
        where I lay pledging my love
           which a banker called in and stacked.
A ball of wine
        to rinse my head
           thrown down on a stomach
Jerking in pain
        to dull my gaze
           screaming and swallowing at the same time
It lasts all night
        Jesus. Why did you do that.

Voice shy and high
        which could once heal me
           as I lay still in its swell and fall
Negligent voice
        which now knows
           no words of love at all.

I run to and fro chittering
over food stores and warm textiles
so slowly gathered. My repeatable space,

my paradise for a woman to lie down in
                                    eyestrings taut with rage, feeling over
my empire of symbols
                my chain of naval bases
                            my deep chambered space of literature,
my non-central court stylemes
                    my cascade of mirrors,
                                  my labyrinthine clarity
my heaps of dust and insects
                    my cabinet of rarities,
                            my folio of preciosities
suspicious and microscopic
                my dated chat-up lines, my copper tracking
                            feed on distorted carcasses
to compose a singular vision caught
and recited by the judges ANXIOUS AND INSIGNIFICANT
wisps of wool, dusty grains EGOISTIC AND OUT OF TOUCH

I tear it down to keep them back
It denounces my thoughts acts and looks
in my voice
scrabbling at bird bones and dead wingcases

I stand guilty of what was stolen from me.
I am fit to be employed
in this scouring of shame and grief.
If
I perceived you, the most beautiful thing
with these same senses
and this capacity for mistakes
I mistook
the rare and precious object of knowledge
fit to be written down; and it passed over me.

Virtual Machines

Something about abandoned machines,
the suspension of life
without immediate decay
            —evokes a mix of fear and hope.

Rail-walking the perspectives, you can trace
the light back to its source, as space
caught in clumps before being folded out.
A vast machine hall, splashed with a ton of
frozen molten metal, we wander separately around
where we were once matches for each other's wishes, projecting
out of our paired and listening bodies
rare and repeated acts to replenish the virtual.
Stopped still in the engine that rolls Time,
the bolt of a day half done with split shapes
stained with crotal, cadmium, and cinnabar,
run over the dies of transparent aperiodic complexity;
half plain, grey stock that becomes everything by dividing.

She thought I was too stupid to suffer much.
Anatomy not learnt on cadavers
lets fingers feel the salt and shining gates
of maximum pain.
Nerve clusters on a symbolic array
turn the skin sac inside out
like gutting a catch:
a surge of bright sensation
where faculties work simultaneously
to replicate damage.
A woman's touch.
Is loss the acquisition of a concept?

Our old codes of finesse and asceticism
suspending stones to give the tremors power,
turning what was clay into china, mark
the massed arrays of movement and knowledge
with that delicacy and smoothness
which leave a wake of paused light as one passes
—I know they do, I used to be loved
by a woman of such price
it strained my faculties

to possess what lost me and to lose
what exceeded me.

The disciplines roll on when the soul is burnt out.
I've studied so many broken machines
scanning the swatches to tell off the flaw in the generator
from the flaws in the pattern.
The years
the years that pin was good for.

The pearls, the sparks, the paired ripple
of the shaking
as it swallows all, mimics all, animates all, changes all,
perfect loss and edgeless shine.
I set in the extensive wreckage of my fine hopes
the calm of steady gazing at objects for their nature,
collating knowledge in stores untouched by shifts,
a thermally neutral bin, lagged to have no outside.
In the hole left by attachments
I pour the golem skills of fact.

Instructions to an actress

You do paranoia *this way*. A facial discipline
of rigid secrecy under which sheer fright
peeps out.

In exercise four
the mention of a place in the street where she used to buy her dresses
fills you with misery and rage
lasting a day. The world wired up like a piano's
naked sinews shuddering and corroding, the window
a single word pulsing. Written on a brick lying on a deserted site,
fills me with misery and rage
I just said that. *Written on a brick slewed in a deserted site,*
painted on the stanchion of the railway bridge.
The railing voices swooping out of dirty air
carry down what you repeat.

Enraged by the young and humiliated by the old, you
turn every quality into measurement, point of honour
deride as you lose it every contest as
exterior, alien, and not counted.
Draining and ejecting
down to a tiny bloodless thing
you spray hateful language; recognising
your like in every room you enter.

In exercise six you carry through the streets
a burning heap of rags on which you expose
your cherished ideas and feelings to a throng who turn
on their heel to disparage and mock and amuse their companions,
saying, Oh, I heard that from someone else.
Exchanging poems for pennies, for the rest
burn and smear them in the street.

Neapolitan-Stanislawskian who asks "why" and then "what was it like"
and then "why" and then "what was it like";
diva loosening shoulder muscles to free the voice
after gathering wild garlic from the woods by Whetstone Stray.
Luci, don't ask me any more questions.
Is there an object I can focus on?
does this remind you of something in childhood?
The draining of the fluid of social life.

A shaking in the air where everyone else sees
what you can't. Your owned glimpse
of something ancient, elaborate, and wholly alien
governing the movement of people towards each other.
You break off part of its design—
overcoded, teeming, charged with pattern—
that grows blank as it cools.

The actor in three planes
developing a kinetic mask
using animals as unit structures:
a movement for each cube of the room,
a clock face where you can note the end of gestures—
to show the human race itself in a space guarded by truth and darkness.
The speed of recovery of balance in walking
loops from which Time flows
shapes uttering in hundredths of a second
physiognomy in muscles of the back and eye
—till all is said without the actress moving.

A neuromuscular sequence
set to a structure drill
15, 16, 17
28, 29 30

another 10 for luck
all over my living room

I defy the ordinance of all secular instances
with a *fin de non recevoir*. Eloquent and untouched,
I slight and set aside learned opinion, literary
taste, government, the course of assimilations.
In a landscape damped, baffled, and razed
I call society to its trial and freeze its accounts.

The second sight and myopia of anxiety
as you lose balance and sway from the knees
see things minutes before they happen;
the scrabbling at tiny insects of flaws
becomes the gift of abstract thought.

Take up reacting late and as if with effort
find repetitive, modular, undemanding tasks
that conceal the slackness and bring you sleep.

An aura, an alarm,
a blank climax evaded in still flight.

Just cut—
as the music of collusion strikes up,
the cubes of pure space
burst between two voices—
one spiral of intolerance, rage and indifference.

An inch you wish less than any other
a mean fabric soaked with the fluids of the self
a portable plot
realised in every social space
that others scuff the borders of;
you square shoulders. growl. glare. hackle.
of inane vigilance puny commands.
A solitary smell.

A mimicry of movement at the wrong speed
a shell that can neither act or react,
courteous at breaking strain. Whatever can be frozen,
fixed, pinned, compelled, immobilised, injuncted
makes you calm;
shifts, thaws. Slides, slurs.
The beautiful past frozen with her face in a smile.

The sight of other people in love makes you stiffen
—in shock, vacancy, agape, as if alone.

Tune grasped, split and sequenced
the intelligence that flickers over the body
the space that we create by moving through it
the play by which we realise what we are about to be.

Adesso non posso

The light rendering space erases and floods the brain
the sight of a noble torso and breast
luring something from its deep and dark sleep
to wake for a period of minutes.
A doorway through which a new self comes,
a room in which I came about.

A Sunday morning in 1963,
the screen on in the sitting room in our house in Loughborough,
I'm seven years old, a beautiful woman in a bedroom,
she starts to take her clothes off, smiles at someone,
her face is full of life, she moves gawkily but with nervy enthusiasm,
I gaze as if pouring myself into the picture, she is down
to a bodice of stiff black lace, and stockings,
my vein system rewiring itself while I watch
the black glamour object giving off blue heat, sheets
of new skin unwrapping themselves like white stars
opening in the tender sky of childhood. Suddenly her face changes,
she says
No I can't
Not now

A smell of something nameless and alive.
My body is soaked, new. The energy
stops at maximum, humming. A hand
picking me up by the hair, crushing and stretching me.
Reshown on my screen, incomplete, *italiano*
the scene shown in a lesson programme, Sunday morning's task,
I worked out as I learnt the grammar of the imaginary
it was Antonioni, the sudden girl with the long legs was Vitti. In 1991
I was queuing beside the Thames for 'La Notte', looking for that scene, for
the completion of the glimpsed, where
a woman too was turned back
whom I saw
sad, vague, excited,
crossing the café area of the concert hall next door, and caught up with,
And later
sketched a transformation scene
And later
completed the lesson
And later
conducted my life

through her gaze equipping frames
in which the desired experience is caught.
An improvisation of opposing actors,
a sift and indrift she searched for weighed patterns,
a polycentric replacing of scenes,
a *dérive* through places and institutions
—she shot her life as the last Antonioni film.
Nine days' queen or,
the decentralisation of the most privileged actions.
Superbly
        empty halls
                we figure.
The women glamorous, the men alluring and disappointing,
this *mise en scène* she embraced
among the commands of the senseless
as modernity.
A space full of exactingly visible order,
geological masses emitting a Time whose recession
swallows us.
Woman who
      before seizing the lover
            writes the parting scene—
I was chosen
      for my lack of substance.

Scenes which after a thousand repetitions we repeat
quite impersonal, on whose lack our character founded;
unavoidably, in pure improvisation and loss of knowledge;
rhythmic, in scattered jags of folly and excess.
We part from desire to find the world disappeared.

Years later fumbling through the cabinet I realised
the type object may itself be a dealer's fine forgery
what we thought was the new lyric poetry
wasn't, on that TV screen in 1963
the one I saw tossing aside the secrets wrapping
a new power and a new chemical state
wasn't an Italian
it was you. A series outside time, recognition
searched out through a looping dark flame,
closed on me. Frames discarded like leaves around a candid core.

Bodiless self-imposing patterns, recursively sought after
where arousal and anxiety spiral and decline
as fixed sequences in the superflux, eject

a psychic anatomy. Vitti in black. Could I rewrite the scenes
I watched when I was thirteen, wandering round a town in Northamptonshire
with cropped hair? was it rehearsing the guilt of others towards me,
repeating gratification, dreams of being a writer? Rolled-up flats
in a huge old barn, waiting to be washed and fitted-up for the strolling
reverie. Roaming because trace minerals missing. Cellular hunger guides
a scanning spiral. The surface geometry of chemicals coded into a dream pattern.
In sleep I dive three miles deep, swimming through passable earth
to swipe at loose treasure. Calm ripples to the point of reflection. A room stacked
                              [with reels of cinema without the silver.
Light up the arc, and project a few frames. Eat
that dark, scarce, infinitely compacted light smeared on a stone wall.

Before waking I possessed you again,
a star tearing through my roof. Surfacing
through a heated lake
where I would have said,
Love, clutch these moments rushing of the night
catch this burst of heat, love,
fall as this scarlet hour falling

draws on shame terror repining.
Opulence and admiration sign inverted,
rage eye, vanishing point, projection source.
The day erased by 8 a.m., exhausted,
a round of idleness and vagueness.
1994. When I think
I get ill.
Strip me down
Scavenge my parts. I remember
to sign on.
Chastity, Diligence, Thrift: a new system
for a lyric poet.

A rich sensibility, a plane of ardent ideals,
where my exclusion is the entry of the aesthetic.
A fantasy relinking thousands of module scenes.
The consort of kitsch
concealing the adored anxious object
under a surface of powdered twirls.
entre colchas de carmesi

Between sheets of white hollands
And silk quilts of crimson
Maria Fernanda was singing

Pining and Peaked

Aisles of the produce of all climates
and presents fit for feasts
where I saunter with my basket open
and part my skin, mingling myself
with Wiltshire cheese, olive oil, meat pies.
So soon as I trust it I recall that trust I gave,
it turns to hurt inside me.
Teeth open me out, I cut it out. Illustrations of my body
wrapped rejected on the shelf.

Desire torn in a place torn in pieces
I see body parts sheared ground up and mutilated
the bursting of skin, the defacing
of its holding in swill acids.

Defeated by
        the coup of psychic co-ordination
                    which the graceful and *dégagé*
Toss off with pleasure
        simply feigning attachment
                to a flirting jar of saffron
A tonal range and lightness
        of touch we know
            means they are liked by women

Scholarship of angst on flaws
        where a peephole skin cell
            is blown up a millionfold
Poor eating habits
        staged celestial lighting effects
            in a hagiographical setpiece
Letting a second world
        slide through its fossil glow
            a darkened disproportionate order.

Coaxing, stroking
talking calmly and cosseting.
The buildings rush past and the trees
whirl around my head
Sweat trickles down my back as I
try to stand upright, stain
my face with composure.

Some velvet morning when I'm straight

I want to buy a filing cabinet and an overcoat.
Post mortem tomography of sick brains
sees unreason. Swallow this.
Altering state above the nose
fixed by glands under the cortex
a capful of bad musk less which
the world would show plainly.
Basildon Tarasque
                shares the kitchen secrets
                        of tainted meat.

A besetting illusion where
my wrist can't turn the doorhandle.
Something
small and flavoursome like an olive
I drink every morning
while waking from cocoon endorphin stupor.
Optical flaw from the chemical fabric of the lens,
reesty sullen fingerling plucked from punkwood and sliced up fine.
On a spectrum
between ramsons and total debility.

Failing now, sides falling in as sticks burned
to fend off the northern chill;
symmetry asserted
as the accumulation of substance in one sealing
is run off.
My shoulders too weak to sustain the child
planar swaying
as I from bowing to pick her up
straighten, in a curve;
a syllable
minim
dip of unsteadiness. The child is frightened.
Clear, I can't support her, if I speak
I waste her time.

I stoop, she clings on to my back
I straighten through a curve whose wavelet
tells her about strength of strings
and a person is not a safe place.
Is my love as weak as I am?

An aura? the colour the air catches? a scent?
Between the man she loved
and one she despised
not even an ounce
or a word lost from my speech.
The shift was
too fine to be reached by study, wasn't there, was
too tenuous to be held back,
changed me from silk to coal.
If it was a small shiny flake of metal
I could say, look, it's burnt to ash,
it's complete.

You lost it. Where did you lose it?

Looks like luxury and feels like a disease

He begs for a large view, he begs for needles.
He begs for a faceless coin, he begs for the heel of a loaf.

He begs not to be looked at. He begs
For a bag of mixed sweets, for wooden joints starting. He begs
For a holding of singles in shoeboxes, and for an Amstrad word processor
[with a ZX81 chip.

He begs for a shirt from Camden Lock Market and a pair of old shoes.
He applies for countenance, aficionados and copycats.

He begs for a bag of apples and a bag of onions.
For a bus ticket to High Barnet and to win arguments.

He forages without shame.
Who now is our cause of laughter, who
Is faint when the bill arrives?
Who eats his own leavings?

He begs for milk and tea, or for fine yellow linen.
He begs for the scrapings of the pan,
And for long yards of red beer.

He solicits for the accord of prestige,
He begs for a shirt, and the holes in it.
He desires greasy victuals. He indents for
Formulae of release on sheets of lead.

He begs for silver foil as snug ticking.
He begs for a door-post when he sees it.
He picks more than he leaves.
He wants an ear for what knowledge he has.

He begs for place spiritual and temporal.
He begs a button for his coat.
He begs to be sick when he is well.
He begs for butter on hot lentils some times around.

He begs for an overcoat frayed at the cuff,
And for tears at the pockets and at the hem.
He begs for a looped passage of water
Under many tall blackthorn bushes

He begs for a setting at the board, and to be privy to counsels.
He begs for expertise, and for a pleasing eagerness.
He likes his facts soft, his
Several sorts of data set out in one picture.

He wishes something for being nothing.
He tenders blank looks and the hollow of his hand.

Money for jam. Just the facts ma'am. Start me up. Pummel my lights,
Unfuddle my wits. A middle term plan. I'll be your man.
Two hands and a tongue. Fealty for sweets. More than a tease and less
Than a sneeze. Eight slices of brown bread. Many penny benefit.
Dosser stipendiary. Largesse of nobility. Decentred penalty.

Laid off solidary, don't take on so. Feet on the loose, heads
On the block. It's a big break, splurge these takings.
Self image no feature. Headstrong avenger.
Scavengeable loser. Illiquid vanguard.
Licensed for languor. What *makes* today's homes
So modern? the purely ornamental people.
No, Sophia, we must wait for the sea to refill.
Cavitation bubble. Stuck to the pan. Pits in the metal.

Qualms at the till. No! to the frill. Part of your charm.
No-hope on a rope. Sloven up in arms.
Slip-ups from the trickledown. The say-sos of the so-said.
Slash to the bone. Stop at home. Artless Goth that nobody owns.
The counter staff sluice you through and out like droppings.
Get your intellectuals here, eight ounces a year. Cleaning
Duties included. Blank in a sweepstake, straw in a haystack.
Hay for wire and gorse for winter. No gain,
No pain. Great feckless Midlands lump.
Mouse soup in Flesh Hovel Lane. Pauper's traps, *de beaux draps*.
Put on your good clothes and write a poem. Gather fuel for an electric kettle.

Crusty old thing. Nowt for tat but lenience at that. A small fortune,
Chastity and thrift. Ditchwater on draught.
At the curt beck of the celestials we raise the Castle of Indolence.

In the Rawheel Café, where the claimants become clients,
The grate of the chicory in the coffee,
The thickness of the waitress's Kurdish accent,
Surpassed the merely generous and comforting.
Talk was cheap and geniality filled the stomach.

Collection towards the definition of a word

An extensible surface that
shapes what it encloses
contains the office of "king"
expands and depletes
is decorated with trophies and capital works
asks in fair words the passer-by's time.

The EYE
of a child in Australia in the 1950s, too-intelligent
not to catch
her father's business system and try it out
glimpsing a thousand factors at once, building
a toy of what rules the country breaks
and follows. She watched
the British firms pulling out and the Americans
taking over "everywhere"
the next generation of profits and knowledge.
Ingorge power by the
signing of your own name to debts.
The bags of coin pass out to the camps of line workers.
Negative space of spoil heaps in the desert
counts the dirt of your capital worth
before you're digging money out of the ground.
The land surveyor traces the line of a cut through a wall of rock,
the cost draughtsman prices up the schedule of works:
a straight metal stroke across an alien planet.
Who builds the headworks and lays the road to the coast
takes the minerals.
A central biotic swelling proved not infinite
by the fluids of the periphery, telltales that draw a turn, surf, and effacement.
Where the scene is animated and impelled, the relations of diameter
and aperture fill the whole oceanic network
of wharves, depots, clients, merinos, accounts, estates, fleets.

You lied to your bankers, and sterling has softened.
There is no core, no
assured exchanges to nurse your strength, no reserve
of captive experiences.
In the runoff
the unsold stock is prized for its pictures.
Go to the technical and debt-fed edge
or write up the grand-paternal cabinet of antiquities.

Calm in hiding, long poems on small subjects,
water spreading across a floor.
Instated by their own judgements, overeating their words
in routinised rollout. After thirty years under hedges
and up trees, sworn judgements break in the cold. The valid mark
stands out on the forehead. Where the stranger stood and maligned you
a white wand effaces a social script as we watch,
To the vindictive the jurisdiction!
To the contemptuous the prestige!
They need just you to give a sermon in Westminster Abbey,
and to buy a hundred pictures for the Tate.

Sumatra Uganda Ceylon
In '42
the fleet of the East Indies Station withdrew to African bases
to clear the wipe-out on post by the Japanese.
Off the Thai coast and in harm's way
a battleship and a battle cruiser
waking a deceit of menace
broadside on to the arc of air-fired torpedoes.
Root of title refuted in due form.
Self-referential markings of
the sea that cannot be impassable or possessed, a feat of reason
ejected by rules and limits to information
storing past games. Great space, pure space
generated by rolls of numbers:
the short and long decay curves called ballistics,
the shell wrapped in the destroyer;
vector-burn of coal and fulminate caps,
echelons of ranges and velocities.
Later,
forward raiding of their depots on Sumatra
as seaborne infantry moved through Burma to the Straits.
Cut convoys, rice gorged with seawater, crab reaches as esplanade,
an army dying of starvation sparing the gunshots.

Controlling Asia through a micrometer in Lancashire,
millwrights making the tools that made the unjamming machines
from gauge scorings to *Weltraum*. Someone scratched
the years the mills would run from when the Pennine streams
were first impounded in their risings
to when the whole town banked a cold at its hearth.

A net of black thread
shaped by what it excludes,
cast round what is half-
inner half-outer, a spectral investment,
a tin chest of estate papers.
A set of references in real space
finding the edge between In and Out.

Shape, the Shape of Shared Space

A hand full, a hand spills
the Pelagic Stone, hard and sullen
hurting your fist
made of speech compacted
A philosophising, sarcastic, moaning, jewel.

A fetish object
I cherished. I slept on. I drew on paper. Saw
the revets of its cyclical polygons
flashing onto blank surfaces.
Pounded in my shallow dreams taking a thousand shapes.
Turned my limbs into marble, wet silk, malachite, torn steel, sea-foam.

It was a crystal whose interior
turned round perfect vertices
was a smooth white cube.
Plane edges reach upwards like the chimney of a drying-house,
orthogonal profiles slot together to create space,
spokes of curved chambers radiate
recession of transverse octagonal beams.
Its surface was made of molecules of words
tumbling and springing, snapping back
over and over without breaking the skin.

It draped and sealed us as we walked together down the streets
of a bored, contemptuous, extravagant town,
kicked passers-by into the gutter.
The bronze of plates and the green reaches of the canal
played its potent song across the fermenting waste of the market.
We followed its most perverse commands.

But then one day
you threw it away
this salt-dripping, optically scattered, hunk of heat.
I couldn't speak
but looked at the space where you had gone.
I clenched the jewel to my body, fondled, swallowed it,
said the same words to it a million times.
Paff. It wears a hole in my head and
rolls out into the light, spinning to shake the blood off.
Slurp. It wears a hole in my stomach and falls out

wet with pap and spew and grindings.
It took on a snakeskin surface
ribbed, dappled, smoked, chill to the touch
and as I lie here it speaks to me.

Find the most stupid job in the directory
Do it till you die
Find the most stupid woman in the city
Take her until she sees through you
Find the dullest voice in the language
Try to memorise it
From now on the only feelings you can have are in drink.

I say, I'm not allowed to drink.

Old money, this jewel
fixed in a photo spread in *Gracious Living*
citable from a *catalogue raisonnée* from the Munich specialists
details inventoried and stored in the solicitor's strongroom
provenance established through a Turcoman tribe, a Byzantine treasury, a
                                            [princely grave near Kerch
its past owners the most instructed and the most ignorant.

Five eyes are fiver than two

sound to which we reduce our silence
skylight through which we
draw down virtual extents to elicit our behaviour

the emptied torso catching and patching together
fine lengths of instructions
going round where spores and pollen swirl
the shell which seizes its organs from others.

A surmise
that the setting of fine movements
in a fixed and elaborated order
syllables we thrill
whose theme too high does seem
for stored neuromuscular firing rhythms
sets up and off
the relief of unhappiness

a shop selling ephemeral commands
written in a spiral along a paper cylinder
a different colour for each hour, insets
of Chinese sages with their wandering staves

learning Welsh vocabulary and doing push-ups
a fat Methodist novel
full of fiery heartenings and steady declines

or a set of films from mouse eyes
cups of moonlight
unadapted to the sun's
richer celestial glut
of light inaccessible; a headache flows in through the wide lens,
it couples to a mouse brain and movement control,
the ringed stabiliser and deformable skull;
an auditory fluid inhabited by different periodicities.

A stall genre
written by unemployed classicists in the tavern quarter
where the lovers sing in Nanjing dialect, the servants tattle in a racy Shanghai
[dialect,
and the policemen stumble over a mediaeval Peking dialect
the finale has to employ
an adequate number of dancing girls
their profile prolonged by feathers

The Shield of Perseus

The colour of silence
neurological shimmer, the density of the air
fine silver needles about to shake.
A kind of drink called the *fins écarts*, or
sequence rules for reading a room—
A forestallers' viewing of
                mondain intelligentsia,
                              skincare of the selfware,
The popular front of lurking
                aesthophanous autonomarchs
                        and gainsaying exquisites,
writing to the script which writes
                an invisible public score, or,
tautologous honorifics
            from spoils to favours—
plucking tender leaves
            of competitive morality.
Me too
        spinning steadily
                to impress one's rivals
I'm one of these happy few.
The phantom of beautiful language
is tempted by the space they stress
and lock as offsets are defined as peaks.

On the shield I watch my actions
at 0.5 second's delay, stiff and shiny,
a screen of warrantable optic quality,
holding five minutes of extent, a graphic
alloy scanning grain edges & wave apices.
My facial planes heaving in
vagueness over a
rigid gaze of horror brightened by
swells of rage where a
mime of benevolence
is momentary and sinister.

As with languid scruples the buffet of assets
is seized and flaunted
by solicitors of the self and power grocers
he rehearses and rejects an utterance

before a panel probing for flaws of drafting.
Wearing the teeth of deceased professors,
reciting paradoxes in blocks of 7 and 13 syllables,
they set him out and cut him down.

Visible tremor of limbs
where discordant states flow over a shared surface
between a fit and a trance
he sets out his stall once more.

The discretion of women, like an aromatic. This pointless task
of being unhappy proves
the staging of a conversation
with plebeian effort
                    to such attractive victims
                                        of low-altitude blurts.
"I've got it now, a thousand
acts of petty vindictiveness become
a millimetrical
scale of nuances,
the ego enriched by fine scars
into a frill?" At this point
no-one wants to be standing near him.
Social life
now starts some years of obligate recess.

Starved by the feast at
seeing two other people in love
She experienced the moment of aura and admired herself experiencing it
where the desire to imitate them
makes all the litigation files start reciting at once
a tragedy no larger than a bath.

Commerce and local advantage

Big flat dredge barges with their rusty towers
grab the silt and gravel from the drowned ground;
balky Amsterdam craft with pelican mouth, on stork legs.
The seagull's sweep is wider than the shear-tower's pivot.
The spark volley, from the welder's nozzle where he
perches on a step thirty feet above the Thames, spreads
plunging towards the change of colour, as
slight outset differences are exploded by the
red spatter cone stopped by a disc of water.
The liquid state is remembered in freeze as uniformity of shape—cf.
a shot tower. Where height acts like objectivity.
and certainly in these tall buildings,
on the riverine banks of artifice towards Saint Paul's, values are made.
Troping on size we swivel to the
head frill of a lizard display, extends opened gorge
snarl threat of apparent twice-size,
a lexical unit of human art. Achilles vibrating his weapons,
erectile tissue, a fake head in blow-up.
Richesse of flow unhooked from fleshly referent.
Threat display all over the video shop window. Holding
guns as if erections were too small for their fists. Congested
body tracts squeezing the brain. I try to signal something not size and sexual
[readiness *and*
I wouldn't mind taking out Neil Astley with a Heckler & Koch, catching
Peter Forbes in the open with a Glock nine mill,
freezing Seamus Heaney with a long-barrelled Ruger.
The anus is a key innovation and not everything has one.

A greasy Armenian bole or clay
to turn the chalk a red flesh colour, or
when a gall wasp has laid in the oak bud, the cosseted infant swollen and
[fledged
takes to the air, leaving a nut rich in acids, decayed body parts
hungry for iron, mixable as inks, the priciest from Aleppo.
Every creature and every quarter searched
for what is excellent of its kind.
A city is an artefact which makes itself, a
honeycomb stuffed with competing hypothesising agents
differentiating inwards, as the foliage of a tree, slanted
to catch light, swerving
like paddles on a millwheel spaced and
offset snapping up

droplets as dapples tumble in layers,
a circlet whose sum is darkness.
Souk of a hundred shops where wrists and tongs work
many manhours in a wafer of few kilograms.
Pounced with an agate or touchstone burnisher
the soft hair of squirrels and goats
minerals from earths and ores,
dyes from turmeric, bark and dried flower petals
minute emeralds and rubies.

Wages and unemployment go up together.
I can't get back
in those rooms where movements
are swift, light, and perplexing.
Progress towards simultaneity, the inexplicit, the density of
learning, depth of skill, high specification
segregates the less adapted adapting into
low cost labour: *het grauw*. The swarm of innovations
developed in years of experiment, no income,
originality from the striving to dominate and into crankiness,
includes the one nobody wants, also low priced effort.

Pages of skin she turned over in a shop
holding words that made her eyes go bright
or skin flush pink, passing on knowledge
which set in a matrix of prices at auction,
patter of prizers, extensive sampling,
regional flavours, auras of provenance, chemical curves,
taught her the exact nature of the object,
induced her to leave.

I penetrate the big space of
the Science Reference Library off Chancery Lane,
catch my breath, in a spin as I stabilise my head with
priming, cavitation bubbles, entrained air separating
at speed, swash plates, tip-swept blades, backwash,
head and fall, throughput, viscosity, fallout.
And I am happy
that most engineering fluids have a Newtonian flow
because liquids should not drop out of an eternal present,
not crawl up an energy slope, in quasi-memory.

Crossing the Grand Union, I walk down Weighbridge Road
from my parents' home to an industrial estate
asking KBS Pumps, Let me

43

translate your German technical documents.
Words are the edges of a situation,
prose hammered till its native ambiguity
vanishes in clear This-Thats like the devices themselves.
What separated dry land from water on Day One
dropping the periodic land between the two rivers
must have been a pump of the Delta type.

The manager talks me through the sheds,
my eyes popping with CAD libraries, proliferants,
OEMs, factory originals, unique implementations,
data pipes, translation snags. I scan the tangle
and design an information system for them on my feet,
a job which

he offered me there and then. I stop at home
waiting for the call. I want
a light industrial estate, I come from the Midlands, I need
a corporation and a computer storage system
plugged into my connector plane
to make me calm. The third part of your brain
do you know where it is?
Acting out the things I believed as a child.
Headquarters in Germany wouldn't come through with a count head.

Fields above Turin where the canals
use some kind of Alp for the head of water
and a cut-up blue plastic sack as the floodgate
the mother of all switches, cheaper than wooden slats or hatches.

Sometimes in the game, two hearts don't feel the same.
One heart's got to choose and one heart's got to lose.

The technique of visualising

Raise both scene and characters
at blurred speed, in dazzling detail, with an internal past, with organic shading,
proper motion, in pinnacled steep recession
more consistent than truth, my heart knocking as
I embrace the dark lovely smoke, my veins
swollen with fumes. An intact cognitive line
surfaces on a pulse to raze what I recite and see,
cheating memory; the head which clears it made
from the same flesh as the error,
height in depth; at their juncture I grow dizzy and fall
and depth in height where reason wipes down to the grey shaking core.

Bleachprint.
No scene, no characters.
A carnal eye tracking on shifting ground.
This bliss, and terror durable as a jittering hand, I
added to the created world.

The big music of a hundred people working in exact
division of roles at highest strain, characters effaced and elevated.
A management graphic where I draw
a phased model of national revival and *roll'em Pete*.
Nets bright with fish. Stocks cleared at list price.
Messages pass, cut and winged, dripping unshared meanings.
A drama, a course to run, a colour or ambience
shaken out
a rapid succession of states
reshaping their human components and being reshaped.
A set of rules in every building,
botany of 700,000 firms as partite entries
in a Linnaean table kept in some State institute.

So many fish in transparent water
swirling, no two following the same path,
constrained by other paths. How to record
the whole? not seizing the line of local movement
until the plan is there. Opening cold bright guts for their message,
scooping out the narrative mud on the seabed, counting
the birds where they dive on churned water at the back of a wave.
Draw up a net full of fins and eyes.
Fitting a thousand pieces into a pattern, one piece
into ten patterns.

There was a sludge in the pillars where an engineer
sank a gauge telling the pressure on the bearing frame,
checking the statics of a building holding 500 people,
system telltaled at a single point as if aware.
I open a hatch and the speed of a fluid tells me
how the *economy* is? The volatile luck sap
bulging and overflowing in shop windows, trade ads, lorries rushing by.

I bear the epoch on my shoulders. No, in a shopping bag.

A door saying JOB CLUB above a white goods shop where
a small intense man tells us, there are 5 million people looking for work,
it's the 1840s, Marx knows the rules again, the bosses
have it just how they like and you've to be who they want.
A woman breaks down in sobs, he quietens her
vision and fear of her fellow-citizens
before telling us we can't resist him. Not on
round about forty-five quid a week. Show me your CV.
At two choices, of taking his group to the streets
and storming the government seat of Barnet, or foretelling
victory through subservience, he shouts at shared doubt
as if trying to boil a pond by body heat. Tie
yourself in knots and we'll
pay for the string.

Burnt Eye

Ist zwivel herzen nahgebur
daz muos der sele werden sur.
Plane that flickers between two lights,
jagged sound of two voices I utter,
one calling away the other, one
starting at shadows, bent by swollen veins,
taking grains of dust as clumps of earth,
contradicting itself, sobbing, railing, lying.

The old highly integrated mental objects
refute the science of anxiety,
the straight fall of light adjusts the lens.
The bridges on the Loughborough to Leicester Navigation
described in a resolution of 1791
are well known to me in their present state,
cambered passable hunches kept by blue coving.
The railway bridge carrying the South Leics line across
the Grand Union Canal, on the wolds side of town,
has been unpainted now since 1973,
rust has eaten one of the horizontal I-beams quite through,
flakes of gnawed red iron scattered like old dead bark
a circular wound of stepped sides like an AP impact;
dispersal of bound material,
wear and steeping along the canal bank
where swans took off with creaking racks of quills into the fog;
a riparian row of disused factories, the power belt of the era
when they still had troops stationed in the mill towns.

Ignorant. Egocentric. Boring me with
these callow and opinionated drafts
of unimprovable land
shaping sensitive youths in industrial towns.
Let them eat their canal bank.
No, I show a room
full of the chic, the affluent, and the influential
of good-looking women and available men
trading power and stalking each other
where I blow in late cutting such a flash
that everyone there asks who I am
and everyone else knows.
Too slow! I mean too slow! to be allowed in.

Three Records of the Floating Life

No coffee, no alcohol. No fried food. No wage packet.
In the Rawheel Café
listen to each other as if each word was worth gold
drink each other's coffee and never your own. Recall
the behaviour of damp courses and the economy,
of chickpeas and the French nation. Argue it out
till all knows where each has been.
The clientele had no money. I had the entrée to this circle.

She shed a poem and fled to Wales in the guise of a great eccentric hawk.
A spiral dither
a protective bag almost large enough to climb inside. A set of
theories about bird behaviour. About three feet of jangly dangly
verbal ornaments in screen mode. Intelligence wrapped as
vagueness and alarm. Expectations of the literary life.
Moths flutter—big soft headed furry ones prance happily
about her head. My macintosh has been drinking. My hard disc is
listless and neurotic and has strategies to attract attention.
Sweet lyric fluting of wish to escape. A long
associative stroll through the stalls of fruit and military Bohemian clothes,
a dialogue of lurches, twirls, and wonderfully fine ash. No,
linnets don't always grasp the fact. A wider identity played by ear.
Afternoons in the Sluice Café scoring Big Marks on questions
of romance and political engagement.

Partiya Karkaran-e Kurdistan-e
—the Farsi sufficient for *that,*
under arms or rhetoric on the plateau
edging the Just State
kardan twice with a draft of Western plosives
cadring the mill hands in East Eight.

Completing a
pleting a sentence suspended for three years.
Their attention has moved on to departmental budgets
and the publication lists are closed. Timed out, page swapped.
All my information has been spoken by other people.
My bed yards deep in dust. Too late
to devise an up to date chat line or mend my cotton jacket. An hour of
[bright anxiety
followed by sixteen of sweet blank sloth. Skills rusted. Ideas forgotten.

Hundreds of graphomanic notebooks. Head in pieces.
Too late to develop a presentable surface. Too late to devise controls.
Adapt the domestic sector to the market
as nobody wants your thoughts stop having them.
Moderating anxiety through symbols, through
divisions of time
eating anxiety like slices on bread.

He talks to me
                weakness open to weak patterns
                                about feelings and wishes.
We step into a doorway out of the rain, he drinks a can
there, in an entry, by coloured wall-tiles, before going home.
blue shallow breaks vermilion
I feel a pang of love for this man who
never remembers who is powerful
because of their certificates saved in polyvinyl envelopes,
their salvation programme hung in cabinets,
their Theories carried in matt black heat-resistant metal tubes.
lit rushes and moor-water
You don't steal up on Foundation Money
by being
                unconditionally kind
                          to the unhappy.
The passing man
                vagrant and transient,
                          without office,
balanced light enough to
                be captured by light
                          dissolve in water.
flicker
momentary shifts
                of love and the virtues of materials
cinnabar green deep
skin pouring
            a poetry and music
                    forgetful of division.
We stay dry,
we look at glazed tiles in the doorway, we look out and talk.
There's nobody I'd rather huddle with. *Die Tasse ist unser.*
Relief and security lance in the white rain shooting off Finchley High Road.